Duck Hunting

BY MATT DOEDEN

AMICUS HIGH INTEREST • AMICUS INK

Amicus High Interest and Amicus Ink are imprints of Amicus
P.O. Box 227, Mankato, MN 56002
www.amicuspublishing.us

Library of Congress Cataloging-in-Publication Data
Doeden, Matt, author.
Duck hunting / by Matt Doeden.
pages cm. – (Great outdoors)
Audience: K to grade 3.
Summary: "This photo-illustrated book for elementary students describes duck hunting, the equipment needed, such as a shotgun, duck blinds, and decoys. Includes information on where to hunt and how to stay safe"– Provided by publisher.
Includes index.
ISBN 978-1-60753-798-4 (library binding)
ISBN 978-1-68152-077-3 (pbk.)
ISBN 978-1-68151-018-7 (ebook)
1. Duck shooting–Juvenile literature. 2. Hunting–Juvenile literature. I. Title.
SK333.D8D64 2017
799.2'44–dc23
2015023220

Editor: Wendy Dieker
Series Designer: Kathleen Petelinsek
Book Designer: Tracy Myers
Photo Researcher: Rebecca Bernin

Photo Credits: Dale Spartas/Corbis cover; JD/Shutterstock 5; Tribune Content Agency LLC/Alamy Stock Photo 6; Matt Mills McKnight/Reuters/Corbis 9; Dale Spartas/Corbis 10; Steve Oehlenschlager/Alamy Stock Photo 13; PHB.cz (Richard Semik)/Shutterstock 14; Rich Legg/iStock 16-17; Dale Spartas/Corbis 18; MorozElena/iStock 21; Steve Oehlenschlager/Shutterstock 22; Peter Johnson/Corbis 25; RubberBall Productions/Getty 26-27; USFWS Photo/Alamy Stock Photo 28

Table of Contents

Let's Go Duck Hunting

A gentle breeze blows through the trees. Small waves lap against the shore. Your eyes are on the sky. Suddenly, you spot them. Two **mallards** fly overhead. You lift your gun and take aim. It's a great day for duck hunting.

Mallards are the most common duck in North America.

Things You Will Need

The first thing a duck hunter needs is a gun. Most choose a 12-gauge shotgun. Shotguns shoot **shells** filled with small steel pellets called **shot**. The pellets break out of the shell and spread out to cover a wide area. This gives hunters the best chance to hit their target.

Most hunters use a duck call. It is a little instrument that sounds like duck quacking.

Decoys are fake ducks. Live ducks often land where they see other ducks. Decoys trick ducks into coming toward hunters. Simple decoys made from wood or cork work really well. But some hunters use battery-powered robo-ducks. These decoys even move their wings and heads.

This decoy duck flaps its wings. Real ducks flock together. They may land near this decoy.

A hunter hides in the marsh waiting for ducks. He even makes sure his dog is hiding.

Q How close to a duck do I need to be to shoot?

Ducks have great vision. They usually avoid people. So hunters need a place to hide.

Some people hunt from small boats along the shore. Others build hiding spots on land. These hiding spots are called **blinds**.

A Most shotguns work best within about 35 yards (32 m). Shooting from farther away will hurt the bird, but might not kill it.

The right clothing makes a big difference. Duck hunters avoid bright colors. They wear colors that blend in with the ground. Tans and browns usually make hunters hard to see.

Hunters also want to stay dry. Most wear waterproof clothing. **Waders** are high waterproof boots. They allow hunters to wade into shallow water without getting wet.

Q Should I buy camouflage clothing?

This hunter wears waterproof hip waders to keep his feet dry.

A

Many duck hunters wear camo. But the important thing is that your clothing color blends in with your surroundings.

A good hunting dog likes to swim and can be trained to get ducks.

Q Can I use other dog breeds or mixed breeds?

Many hunters hunt with a dog. A hunting dog will swim out to get any ducks that have been shot. The most popular breed is the Labrador retreiver. They are good swimmers. And they like to fetch objects. This makes training them to be hunting dogs easy. Other popular breeds include springer spaniels, American water spaniels, and Nova Scotia tollers.

A Of course! You can hunt with any dog that is a good swimmer and strong enough to retreive a duck.

Safety First

Duck hunting can be fun, but hunters have to be careful. Gun safety is the first concern. Most hunters take gun safety training. They learn basic safety rules. They learn not to load a gun until they're ready to start hunting. And they learn to treat all guns as though they're loaded at all times.

Gun safety classes are the best place to learn how to handle a firearm.

Hunters work together to stay safe. Many also find hunting in a group is more fun.

Q Are there any safety supplies I should bring?

Hunters are safest hunting in groups. That way someone is there to help in case of trouble. Duck hunting groups have to work together. Everyone must know which direction each hunter is firing. That way they don't end up between a fellow hunter and a duck!

A Bring emergency supplies such as food and water. Pack fire-starting gear and a cell phone in a waterproof bag.

Many hunters use small duck boats. Safe hunters wear life vests in the boat. They do not stand up in the boat. It could tip over. It's a bad idea to wear waders in deep water. If a hunter falls into the water, the waders will fill up. This can cause a hunter to sink.

Q What do I do if my boat tips?

A duck boat is a good way to go to where the ducks are.

A Don't panic. Don't try to turn the boat back over. Instead, get to shore as fast as you can.

Ducks flock together in wetlands. You'll find ducks in marshes, ponds, lakes, and rivers.

Q When is duck hunting season?

Where to Go

The best duck hunting spots are places where ducks come and go. That includes lakes, rivers, and marshes. But hunters can't just go to any lake and start shooting! First they must learn about state and local hunting laws. These rules say where and when hunters can hunt.

A It is different in every state or province. But duck hunting season generally is in fall.

In most places, hunters can hunt on **public land**. These areas are owned by the state or country. Experienced hunters can point beginners to good starting places. But many hunters find their best spots on **private land**. Private land is owned by a person. Hunters must get the owner's permission to hunt there.

Owners of private land may not let hunters use their property.

NO HUNTING
KEEP OFF
All Persons are Forbidden Gunning or Trespassing on These Premises.
Under Penalty of the Law

The right day can make a big difference. Cloudy days are best. Ducks have a harder time spotting hunters when it's cloudy. Wind helps too. Ducks tend to stay close to shore when it's windy. That also brings them closer to the hunters. Many duck hunters say the best hunting is right before a storm.

These dark clouds could bring rain. They are good for hunting.

These girls had a good day of duck hunting.

Have Fun!

Pack up your gear and grab your gun. With a little planning, you'll be ready to hunt. Sit back, relax, and enjoy the fresh air. It won't be long before you hear the flapping of wings overhead. If you are lucky, you might have roast duck for dinner.

Glossary

blind A structure designed to keep hunters hidden from their prey.

decoy An object that looks like a duck; decoys are placed in the water to attract real ducks.

mallard The most common type of duck in North America, known for its green-colored head and white ring around its neck.

private land Land owned by private citizens.

public land Land owned by the government.

shell A case full of pellets to use in a shotgun.

shot Small metal pellets loaded into a shotgun shell.

waders Tall waterproof boots that go up to the hips or chest and keep your legs and feet dry while walking through shallow water.

Read More

Carpenter, Tom. *Waterfoul Hunting: Duck, Goose, and More.* Minneapolis: Lerner, 2013.

Omoth, Tyler. *Duck Hunting for Kids.* North Mankato, Minn.: Capstone Press, 2013.

Pound, Blake. *Duck Hunting.* Minneapolis: Bellwether Media, 2013.

Websites

DuckHunter.net
http://www.duckhunter.net

Ducks Unlimited
http://www.ducks.org/

The Labrador Retriever Club
http://www.thelabradorclub.com

Every effort has been made to ensure that these websites are appropriate for children. However, because of the nature of the Internet, it is impossible to guarantee that these sites will remain active indefinitely or that their contents will not be altered.

Index

About the Author

Author and editor Matt Doeden has written hundreds of children's and young adult books on topics ranging from history to sports to current events. Several of his books have been Junior Library Guild selections and have been listed among the Best Children's Books of the Year by the Children's Book Committee at Bank Street College. Doeden lives on a lake in Minnesota with his wife and two children.